Something You Forgot … Along the Way

Stories of Wisdom and Learning

Something You Forgot ... Along the Way

Stories of Wisdom and Learning

Kentetsu Takamori

Translated by
Juliet Winters Carpenter

Ichimannendo Publishing, Inc.
Los Angeles Tokyo

Something You Forgot ... Along the Way: Stories of Wisdom and Learning
By Kentetsu Takamori
Published by Ichimannendo Publishing, Inc. (IPI)
19750 S. Vermont Ave., Suite 200, Torrance, California 90502
info@i-ipi.com www.i-ipi.com

Translated by Juliet Winters Carpenter.

NOTES TO THE READER:
In the process of producing the English translation, this book was adapted by the author in close collaboration with the translator.
Throughout the book, Japanese names are given in Western order. However, names of historical and literary figures who lived prior to the Meiji era (before 1868) are given in traditional Japanese order, family name first.

Jacket design by Kazumi Endo
Photographs by amanaimages

First edition, September 2009
Printed in Japan
13 12 11 10 09 1 2 3 4 5 6 7 8 9 10

This book was originally published in Japanese by Ichimannedo Publishing in two volumes under the titles of *Hikari ni mukatte hyaku no hanataba* and *Hikari ni mukatte hyakunijusan no kokoro no tane*.

Distributed in the United States and Canada by AtlasBooks Distribution, a division of BookMasters, Inc.
30 Amberwood Parkway, Ashland, Ohio 44805
1-800-BookLog www.atlasbooks.com

Distributed in Japan by Ichimannendo Publishing
2-4-5F Kanda-Ogawamachi, Chiyoda-ku, Tokyo 101-0052
info@10000nen.com www.10000nen.com

Library of Congress Control Number: 2009929449
ISBN 978-0-9790471-1-4

ISBN 978-4-925253-37-6

Contents

1

Making the World Happier

A Smiling Face and a Word of Kindness

John Wanamaker (1838–1922) was a department store pioneer. One day, a young man came to apply for an advertised job opening in his store. Wanamaker himself conducted the interview, and the applicant answered every question with a firm "Yes" or "No." He was a strapping young man with impressive academic credentials, and no one present at the interview doubted he had nailed the job. Even so, Wanamaker turned him down.

"He seemed like a fine fellow," commented one of Wanamaker's aides. "Was there something about him you didn't like?"

Wanamaker explained, "He answered all my questions with a plain 'Yes' and 'No' instead of 'Yes, sir,' 'No, sir.' If he doesn't know enough to be polite to me, I doubt he would treat customers with the proper consideration. In my store, the customer always comes first. I couldn't possibly hire him." The story illustrates the power of a single word.

Wanamaker's employees used to say that one cheery "Good morning!" from the boss was enough to make them enjoy a week's work. Their joy in working translated into booming success for the store. People talk about serving society, but nothing does so much to make the world a happier place as a smile and a cheerful hello. Like a street performer, Wanamaker brought hope and cheer to all around him.

The worst skinflints are those who are stingy with smiles and hellos. All it takes to make others happy is a twinkle in the eye and a word or two, so don't hoard them. The Anglican clergyman Sydney Smith (1771–1845) said, "When you rise in the morning, form a resolution to make the day a happy one to a fellow creature." By doing this for ten years, he pointed out, one could make 3,650 people happy—the equivalent of making a charitable donation to an entire town. That would indeed be an act of charity in keeping with Śākyamuni's teaching to "have a smiling face and speak words of kindness."

2

Stones That Longed to Be Diamonds

Polishing Oneself

Among the stones along a riverbank lay a single diamond. A sharp-eyed peddler saw it, picked it up, and sold it to the king. The sparkle of the new diamond in the king's crown delighted the citizens of the country.

The story of the diamond's success reached the other stones, and caused a furor. They were consumed with jealousy. One day they called out to a passing farmer: "A stone that used to be one of us went to the capital and made a name for himself. He's nothing but a stone, the same as us. Surely if we went to the capital, we could be successful too. Please take us there."

Taking pity on them, the farmer put the stones in his cart and took them along to the capital. Their dream of making it to the capital came true, but the result was far from what they had expected. Naturally, they did not end up in the king's crown. Instead they were made into cobblestones and suffered under a load of heavy traffic every day, weeping tears of bitter regret.

One day, as the owl flew off scowling, his companion the dove called out, "Where are you off to with a face like thunder?"

The owl said plaintively, "The people around here don't like my screech, as you know, so I decided to move."

The dove chuckled and said wisely, "That's no use. Move if you want to, but as long as you don't change your screech, the people at the new place aren't going to like you any better than the people here do. If you're willing to leave the place where you were born, you should be willing to make the effort to change your voice."

Polishing oneself is the true secret of success. If you shine, people will naturally be drawn to you and your life will improve. If you chase after success without struggling to better yourself, you only pave the way to failure.

3

How Much Is Enough?

The Farmer Who Was Overcome by Greed

There is a story by Leo Tolstoy about a land-hungry farmer who heard of a country so vast that land could be had for the asking. He traveled there and found it was true. The inhabitants and the chief all welcomed him, and the chief told him that he could help himself to any piece of land he wanted—as much as he could get around on foot in a single day.

"There is one condition," added the chief. "You must start at sunrise and return to the place where you started before the sun sets. Start anywhere you like and go around marking the corners. Go as far and as wide as you please, but come back on time or you will gain nothing."

That night the farmer lay awake with excitement at the thought of the vast tract awaiting him. In the morning, he set off just as dawn was breaking and soon settled on a starting point for his land. Gradually his pace quickened to a trot.

After going several miles he marked another corner. Eventually he broke into a run, driven by the knowledge that the faster he went, the more land would be his. He came to what would have been a reasonable turning place and passed it by, his greed spurring him on. Finally, surprised to see the sun already high overhead, he marked the last corner and began to run back to the starting point.

He barely took time to eat lunch. By mid-afternoon he was worn out, but he threw off his coat and boots and kept running. The sky was red with sunset. His feet were hurt and bloody and his heart was at the bursting point, but if he collapsed now, all his effort would be for nothing. He ran for all he was worth, his eyes on the goal.

His effort was rewarded, for he made it back just in time—only to fall over stone dead. His servant dug him a grave and buried him in it. In the end, all the land he needed was a plot six feet by two.

Tolstoy's farmer is not alone. Greed kills us all.

4

On the Brevity of Our Ties

Ties in this world last only for a time. We are husband and wife, parent and child, for a short period only. Once this reality sinks in, we cannot help treasuring each moment of our brief association.

5

Counseling the Wayward Student

One Professor's Wise Approach

A certain college professor was loved like a father by his students. One day he invited a student who had been leading an irregular life to his house, and spoke to him as follows.

"These days do you ever call your parents or write to them?"

"Sometimes."

"How many times a month?"

"Once or twice."

"Very good. What kind of things do you tell them?"

"I call them when I need money," came the shamefaced answer.

"Nothing wrong with that. When you're short of money, it's better to rely on your parents than to borrow from friends. Is that all you tell them in your letters and phone calls, that you need cash?"

"Yes," said the student, squirming.

The professor sat up straight, a deep light shining in his eyes. "Here's why I called you over today. I want you to write to your parents once a week from now on. Tell them anything—that you got up early, that you had cereal for breakfast, or pizza for lunch, or Chinese takeout for dinner. Any little thing will do, but tell them all about it, will you?"

The student had such respect for the professor that he did as told without stopping to think about the underlying meaning of the request. His parents, having never heard anything from their son but pleas for money, had been worried about him. Now they could relax, and they were overjoyed. They in turn began to write to him and call from time to time with news about home, and now and then they would send him treats.

The student had been partying hard, but because he couldn't always lie about his behavior, he slowly changed. Once he understood how much his parents cared about him, he began to study harder. In this way, a student with a bad reputation settled down and began to lead a simple, wholesome life—all because of the professor's wise tactic.

6

Living for a Great Desire

Jenner and Smallpox

Edward Jenner (1749–1823) is famous for saving mankind from smallpox. His first love was natural history, and he devoted himself to the study of birds. On learning about the centuries-old scourge of smallpox, he formed a great desire to end the suffering caused by the dread disease.

Jenner became fascinated by anecdotal evidence that men and women who contracted cowpox from milking dairy cows never came down with smallpox. He carefully gathered a large body of such evidence and then went to London, where he became a pupil of John Hunter and sought his advice. Encouraged by the great doctor to pursue his dream, he performed many experiments and observed the results with the greatest of care. His confidence grew.

His breakthrough came on May 14, 1796, when he took pus from the hands of Sarah Nelmes, a milkmaid infected with cowpox, and deposited it in scratches on the arms of an eight-year-old boy named James Phipps. This was the first-ever case of what we now call vaccination.

Once Jenner had assembled rock-hard evidence of the efficacy of the treatment, he published his findings—and stirred up a storm of criticism. Some of his opponents claimed that people inoculated with cowpox would grow horns. Jenner responded calmly and patiently to all protests, sparing no effort to improve the welfare of society and mankind. In the nineteenth century alone, tens of millions of lives were saved. Finally, in 1979, the World Health Organization declared smallpox officially eradicated from the planet.

Benefactors of mankind whose great deeds earn them a place in history are inevitably motivated by an intense desire to see their vision come true, and they make ceaseless efforts toward that end, come what may.

7

Ah, Now Their Water Is Gone

How the General Saw Through the Enemy's Ploy

"One arrow can be broken, but not three bound together." Japanese warlord Mori Motonari (1497–1571), a master of wiles and trickery, is famous for this legendary advice to his three sons. After fighting in his first battle at age twenty-one, he went on to fight another 225 battles, great and small, over the course of his adult life. This works out to an astonishing four battles per year.

What was the result of all this fighting? Originally a lowly castellan with a meager income, Motonari ended up ruling the entire western portion of Japan's main island of Honshu.

Once when Motonari went on the attack, he simply surrounded the castle, sat back, and waited for the water supply to run out. The castle lord, a man named Aoya Yubai, was himself a brilliant strategist. One day he brought out his horse and began to wash it with rice in plain view of Motonari's army. From a distance, it looked as if he were washing it with water. Some of Motonari's key retainers advised a change of tactics, but the general brushed their words aside.

After a few days, Motonari sent an envoy into the castle grounds, and Yubai received him cordially. "I am extremely fond of horses," he said. "Let me show you some of my finest." He had five or six horses brought out, along with buckets filled to the brim with water that he proceeded to use to cool the animals off and rinse out their mouths.

When the surprised envoy came back and reported this unexpected development, Motonari responded, "Ah, now their water is gone." He tightened the siege, and Yubai surrendered shortly.

Motonari had the insight to see through the enemy's wily ploy. He was certainly a man of keen natural gifts, but he polished his ability with unstinting efforts. Late in life, looking back over his career, he made this telling comment: "I never relaxed, not even when asleep."

Behind the path
Where many go,
Blossom-covered hills.

8

Take Him the Money Now!

Show Appreciation Immediately

A very wealthy man who suffered from a hopeless illness began miraculously to improve. When he was nearly well, he summoned his steward and ordered him to take ten thousand dollars to the physician, with his deepest thanks.

The steward protested, "Why now, sir? Why not wait until you have made a full recovery?"

"No, I want it done right now. When I was in despair of my life, I thought with all my heart that if only he cured me, I would gladly give him all I owned. Then, once the crisis was over, I changed my mind. 'Nobody does a foolish thing like that,' I told myself. First I decided half would be plenty, then a third. My attachment to my possessions grew and grew. It's a physician's job to heal the sick, I thought; nothing extraordinary about that. People die all the time anyway, despite receiving the best of care, so if I do get well who could say it was his doing? It began to seem that making some outsize gift to him would only make me look ridiculous. If I wait till I'm fully recovered, I'll end up refusing to pay him a red cent. I'm likely to let my bill go unpaid until he insists, just so I can squeeze out all the interest possible. I don't want to turn into such an ingrate. Even though I'm still bedridden, take him the money now!"

When we ask someone for a job or another favor, we are generous with smiles and flattery. We are positive at the time that we'll never forget how much we owe him or her, but as time goes by, gratitude fades to indifference. People who offer sincere thanks to benefactors will succeed; those who forget others' kindness will lose their reputation.

9

The Poor Window Frame

An Inspiring Glimpse of a Mother and Child

This happened once when I was riding a train on my way to give a speech. The car interior was spacious and quiet, with many unfilled seats. Feeling relaxed, I settled back and opened up a book I'd brought along. After a while, tired from reading and lulled by the rhythmical vibrations of the train, I began to nod off—only for my dreams to be shattered by an ear-splitting whistle and the metallic screech of brakes. Apparently the driver had found an obstruction of some kind at a crossing.

The shock of the sudden stop threw me forward, but I managed somehow to stay upright. In the same instant, the shrill sobs of a little child rang out. I saw then that the seats across the aisle in front of me were occupied by a young mother and her child, who had apparently been amusing himself by sitting with his forehead pressed against the window pane, watching the scenery fly by. When the train jerked to a stop, the tot's head banged sharply into the window frame. His wails grew louder and more frantic. Afraid he was hurt, I jumped up, but to my relief there was no sign of injury. Then I witnessed a scene so heartwarming that I was deeply touched.

As the child's pain lessened, he gradually quieted down while his mother rubbed his head reassuringly and murmured soothing words: "Sweetheart, that must really hurt. I'm so sorry. I'll rub it for you and make the pain go away. But you know, you weren't the only one who got hurt. The poor window frame did too. Let's rub it and make it feel better, shall we?" The tot nodded, and sure enough, he and his mother together began to pat the window frame.

I felt chastened, for I had assumed she would say something more on these lines: "That must really hurt. I'm so sorry. It's all the fault of this naughty window frame. Let's spank it and teach it a lesson, shall we?" Such a scene is common enough, giving a toddler a vent for his rage and allowing the moment to pass.

All too often when life deals out pain, people respond by searching for someone else to blame. Perhaps, I reflected, we parents implant this response in our children without meaning to. The child is father of the man, goes the saying, and surely parents have enormous influence in shaping the character of small children.

People who think only of themselves and cannot empathize with others end up in the darkness. Those who would enter the shining Pure Land must take the high road of benefiting others as well as themselves, for benefiting others is indeed inseparable from benefiting oneself.

I left the train wishing true happiness to that mother and child with all my heart.

10

The Best-Tasting Dish

Once there was a king who was determined to eat the world's tastiest dish. He gathered chefs from all over, but he had grown so accustomed to fine dining that his palate was jaded, and nothing appealed to him. "None of them can cook worth a damn," he growled. "Find me a better chef!"

His aides were at a loss, until someone came forward and announced himself to be the greatest cook in the world.

"Can you cook food that will satisfy me?" asked the king.

"Yes, Your Highness, although I must ask that first you do exactly as I say."

"Sounds interesting. All right, I'll do it, so go ahead and make the food."

For the next three days, the new chef never left the king's side, but simply sat and did nothing.

"When are you going to cook for me?" asked the king.

"Soon, Your Highness, I promise."

On the third day, when the king was weak with hunger, the chef brought in a simple dish of vegetables. "Here is the world's tastiest dish, just as promised. Bon appétit."

The king fell to ravenously. After wolfing down the dish, he marveled, "I've never eaten anything so delicious in all my life. What is it, and how did you make it?"

"The sauce that makes all food delicious is hunger," replied the chef. "When you are close to starving, any food tastes like ambrosia."

The pleasure of eating comes from the lessening of hunger. Without the discomfort of hunger, the pleasure of fine dining could not exist. The same is true in life: those who avoid suffering cannot experience pleasure, either. True happiness is not for the timid.

11

On Vanity

Vanity is the greatest cause of failure. As we rise in status and come into greater wealth, we begin to look down on others. Puffed with vanity, we see nothing wrong with our behavior. But "the stalk of rice with the most fruit bows the lowest." Any rise in status or increase in wealth must be accompanied by greater humility. We must become like stalks of rice. It cannot be said too often: don't be vain.

12

Perseverance and Ingenuity Are Key

Don't Make Snap Judgments

Ohashi Sokei (1555–1634) of Kyoto always excelled at the game of *shogi,* which is similar to chess. He became the first Grand Master by going to Edo and defeating the monk Hon'inbo Sansa (1559–1623), a celebrated master of the game, in the presence of the shogun.

As the game proceeded, Sansa made one brilliant move after another, until it seemed apparent to the spectators that Sokei was doomed. The only question in their minds was how soon he would throw in the towel. Shogun Tokugawa Ieyasu (1542–1616) watched in breathless suspense. Sokei, however, remained sunk in thought. Minute after minute went by, but still he remained silent and unmoving, arms folded at his chest. Eventually Ieyasu grew bored and left the room to take a bath. When he returned, Sokei still hadn't moved. Deciding he'd had enough, Ieyasu ordered the game suspended until the following day, and got up to leave.

"One moment, if you please." Still staring at the board, Sokei calmly stopped the shogun. Then he reached out and swiftly executed a move of such surpassing brilliance that Sansa could only gnash his teeth, defeated.

"Ruling the country is no different," said Ieyasu, impressed. "It is wrong to make quick judgments. What counts is persistence and ingenuity. This has been a good lesson for me." He praised Sokei highly, rewarded him with a generous stipend, and made him head of the shogi office in the shogunate.

U.S. railroad magnate E. H. Harriman (1848–1909) once lamented, "Much good work is lost for the lack of a little more." A lump of coal is transformed into a sparkling diamond only by standing up to the pressure of the earth for tens of thousands of years. What then are twenty or thirty years of endurance for those who would attain their long-cherished dream of ultimate happiness? In any endeavor, years of ingenuity, determination, and patience are essential to achieve glory.

13

Tell Yourself You Have Just One Arrow

The Art of Focusing the Mind

As the youth standing in the archery ground faced the target with a pair of arrows, the grizzled old master beside him said bluntly, "You're still a beginner. Make it one." To hold two arrows was customary. Why should he, a beginner, use only one? The advice made no sense.

Despite his misgivings, the youth obediently cast one arrow aside. Then the thought struck him, "Now I have only one." He focused all his mind on it, and successfully hit the target. The onlookers erupted in applause, surprised to see one so inexperienced perform so well. Still, the archer puzzled over the advice he had been given. Finally he sought out the master and asked him for an explanation.

"It's simple," said the old man with a twinkle. "Knowing you have a second arrow to fall back on prevents you from focusing on the first. Your guard goes down. Unless you are prepared to stake all on a single arrow, you could have dozens and it wouldn't be enough."

The idea that "if this doesn't work, I can always try again next time" interferes with concentration. It keeps us from devoting ourselves heart and soul to the task at hand, the way the medieval French philosopher Guillaume Budé (1467–1540) devoted himself to his studies. He left all the household affairs to his wife and did nothing but study. Even when the houseboy ran in and cried, "The house next door is on fire! Hurry, you must escape!" Budé never looked up. He said only, "My wife takes care of everything. Go talk to her."

It sounds ridiculous—and yet to be able to immerse oneself so wholeheartedly in a pursuit is admirable. To be absorbed in one thing to the exclusion of all else, focused solely on the goal, makes any task achievable.

14.

A Seed Not Planted Cannot Grow

The Fundamental Law of Cause-and-Effect

One October, a man went on a trip to the East. A cool breeze blew through fields of ripened grain that stretched in waves of gold as far as the eye could see. Nearby a farmer was leisurely at work, smoking a pipe, his face creased in a smile.

Later the man returned to the same country, and found the waves of gold harvested into neat sheaves, lying piled by each house. From within came the sounds of contented conversation and laughter. The man said to himself, "This is a paradise. Imagine that—people here reap a great harvest with no trouble!" He could only envy such good fortune, and went and told his neighbor all about it.

His neighbor decided to take a look for himself. He set off at the beginning of May and arrived to find everyone covered in mud and sweat, hard at work. Thinking this was strange, he finished his business and went home. When he came by the following month, he found people sweating buckets in the hot sun, hard at work as before, with no golden waves in sight and no sheaves, either. He fumed, "My neighbor pulled a fast one on me. This is no paradise—it's a perfect hell."

Hidden in every success story are tears.

A seed that is not planted cannot grow. People ignorant of this fundamental law of cause-and-effect are greatly to be pitied.

15.

Change Irritation to Appreciation

Born with a Short Temper?

A man went to call on a priest for advice. "I was born with a short temper," he confessed. "They say getting angry only makes matters worse and they're right. After I let off steam I feel rotten, and I regret hurting other people's feelings, but by then it's too late. Is there anything I can do to rid myself of my short temper?"

The priest smiled genially. "Well, well, you certainly were born with an interesting item," he said. "If I am to fix it, though, I need to examine it. Do you have it with you now?"

"Well, no," said the man. "I have nothing to be upset about now, so I can't show it to you."

"That's odd," said the priest. "Since you told me just now that you were born with it, it must be somewhere on your person. Don't be shy, just go ahead and bring it out for me to see."

"No," repeated the man, "it's not here."

"Then where is it?"

"When you put it like that, I don't know what to say. Right now it isn't anywhere."

"Of course it isn't. No one is born with a short temper. The next time you start to blow up in irritation, ask yourself where that fit of temper came from. The answer is, it came from you yourself. To say you were born with it, as if it's not your fault, is shirking responsibility."

Patience doesn't just happen, but must be cultivated. It is all a matter of attitude.

Change irritation to appreciation.

16.

On Resisting Avarice

The mentality that fawns on the rich and looks down upon the poor is a great enemy. Write a note of thanks to someone who sends you a case of fruit, but take even greater care to write to someone who gives you a single persimmon.

17.

Building a Reputation for Excellence

The Fruits of Sustained Effort

In the food-loving city of Osaka there is a famous noodle shop. The owner, an astute businessman, always makes a point of stopping in other noodle shops when he travels, in order to try their wares. He asks in detail about the ingredients in the noodles, the soy sauce, and the broth. On returning to Osaka, he carefully compares his way of making noodles with other people's, sparing no effort to perfect the flavor of the product he sells.

One day a customer came from far away to visit the shop, drawn by its reputation. When he went in, he found the owner seated erectly at the counter. To the customer's surprise, before serving a bowl of noodles the waitress would first present it to the owner, who would sample it and then quietly pass verdict. Clearly he lived by an unswerving principle: no customer of his would be served food that failed to meet his standards.

At this demonstration of uncompromising commitment to quality, the man was filled with admiration. A reputation for excellence doesn't come about by chance, he realized, nor does it happen overnight.

Once a man approached the famous musician Sigismund Thalberg (1812–71) with a request for him to perform a piano piece. He was planning to release a new composition, and wished the performance to go well. Thalberg's reply caught him by surprise: "Sorry, there isn't time enough for me to practice."

"Surely a musician as great as yourself can learn a piece this simple in a matter of days," objected the man.

"No," said Thalberg. "I will not perform any piece publicly unless I have practiced it more than fifty times a day for a month, or over fifteen hundred times in all."

These were indeed the words of a master. Such is the dedication of great men. Anyone who seeks to distinguish himself while eating, drinking, and sleeping all he wants might as well look for fish in a tree.

18.

Abuse That Is Not Accepted

Śākyamuni and the Heretic

One day a young heretic approached Śākyamuni and began to heap abuse on him. Śākyamuni listened silently, and when the heretic had finished, asked gently, "Do you sometimes invite your relatives over to your home on festival days and entertain them?"

"Of course I do."

"What if they didn't eat the food you served them? What would you do then?"

"Nothing. The food would just be left over."

"You gave me much abuse just now, but if I decline to accept it, whose will it be?"

"Even if you decline to accept it, it is still yours, since I gave it to you."

"No, for if I do not accept it, you have given me nothing at all."

"Well then, explain what it means to accept or not accept."

"Accepting what is offered means yelling back at someone who yells at you, returning anger for anger, hitting back when someone hits you, or fighting back when someone picks a fight. If you remain indifferent, then you have not accepted anything."

"Do you mean that you never lose your temper, no matter how you are abused?"

Solemnly, Śākyamuni replied with a verse:

"The wise man knows no anger;
Though storms may rage against him,
His mind is placid and calm.
Answering anger with anger is for fools
alone to do."

"I was a fool. Please forgive me." The young heretic prostrated himself in tears before Śākyamuni and swore to follow him.

19.

Promises Are to Be Kept

A young man was taking a walk one day when he came on a shabbily-dressed little girl crouched by the side of the road, weeping as she clutched some broken pieces of pottery. Gently he asked her what the trouble was. It seemed that she was an only child whose only parent was seriously ill. She had borrowed a one-liter jar from the landlord and was on her way to buy milk when she dropped the jar and smashed it. She was crying in fear of a scolding.

Feeling sorry for her, the youth pulled out his wallet and checked it, but he was a poor scholar, and the wallet was empty. "Come back here tomorrow at the same time," he told her. "I'll give you the money for another jar of milk." He shook hands with her and went on his way.

The following day he received an urgent message from a friend: "A wealthy man is here, someone interested in sponsoring your work. He's leaving in the afternoon, so come right away." Yet going to meet the rich man would have meant breaking his promise to the little girl. The young man quickly sent this reply: "I have important business today. I apologize for the inconvenience, but I must ask him to return another day." And he kept his promise to the child.

The would-be benefactor at first took offense, but on hearing what had kept the scholar, he was thoroughly impressed and became his most ardent supporter.

Rich people can be touchy and difficult to deal with. They tend to think that their money entitles them to have their way in everything. Even those who are not rich will all too often break any promise and bend any principle for the sake of money, becoming its slaves.

The Chinese character for "making money" is composed of elements that can be read "trusted person." In other words, money comes to those who are worthy of trust. The basis of trust lies in keeping a promise regardless of its cost to oneself. Promises that cannot be kept should not be made. He who breaks a promise not only inconveniences others but inflicts damage on himself.

20

On Wonderful Fruits

Our struggle is, in the end, a struggle with the self—a struggle that must be carried on. Like muscle training, developing the soul is an extremely painful process. Endure and persevere.

Tangible things may get stolen, disintegrate, break, disappear; the invisible treasure of the soul is indestructible. Whatever pain you suffer will be rewarded in full.

Wonderful fruits will be yours.

21

Gaining a Little, Losing a Lot

How a Farmer Lost His Cow

A farmer hurried along a mountain path at dusk, leading a great cow. The animal evidently was a prized possession of his, for he turned around frequently to check on its progress, and treated it with tender consideration as he made his way home.

Before long a couple of suspicious characters came up behind him. One of them whispered to the other, "See that cow? I bet you I could steal him right now."

His companion shook his head doubtfully. "You're a fine pickpocket, I'll grant you that, but not even you could make off in daylight with a great big cow!"

"Just watch me. I'll show you how good I am." The pickpocket quickened his pace, passed by the farmer and his cow, and disappeared behind a little shrine at a bend in the path.

When the farmer came by, he noticed something lying on the ground. He picked it up and saw it was a brand-new leather shoe. "Here's a find!" he said to himself. "Too bad there's only one. No good without the mate." He tossed it aside and went on his way.

Soon he spied something else lying in the path and picked it up. Sure enough, it was the other shoe. Now if he only had the first one, he'd have himself a fine new pair of shoes. Excited at the thought, he tied his cow to a tree and flew back to retrieve the shoe he'd thrown away. There it was, just where he'd left it. "This is my lucky day!" he exulted. "Imagine getting a fine pair of shoes for nothing!"

He went back full of joy, only to find his precious cow vanished without a trace. All too many people are like him—so distracted by desire for immediate gain that they end up losing what is most important of all.

22

It's Like the Sound of a Pulley

The Wisdom of Socrates

The largest landowner in ancient Greece called on Socrates one day and bragged about his extensive holdings. Socrates rolled out a map of the world and indicated Greece. "Where exactly is your land?" he asked.

"No matter how much land I had, it wouldn't show up here," said the other man, dumbfounded.

"If your land doesn't show on the map, you haven't got much to brag about," said Socrates with a genial smile. "I'm constantly working the universe in my mind."

Socrates is credited with saying, "My advice to you is to get married: if you find a good wife you'll be happy; if not, you'll become a philosopher." There are many well-known anecdotes about his shrewish wife, Xanthippe. Once, hearing her complain all day long about her husband's failure to earn a decent living, a friend of Socrates' commented that such nagging was too much to bear. Socrates rejoined, "I'm used to it; it's like hearing the unceasing sound of a pulley." Another time, annoyed that her husband paid no attention to her litany of complaints, Xanthippe emptied a chamber pot on his head, prompting him to remark, "After the thunder, there generally comes rain." Words like this fend off arguments.

The thought of being saddled with a shrewish wife is aggravating. Think of it as learning to ride a bucking horse, however, and it becomes a challenge. A man who can handle the most difficult horse of all need fear no one. Socrates impressed this lesson on his disciples using his own family life as illustration. This is an important lesson in the art of living.

23

I've Diagnosed Patients Before, But Never Their Money

A Physician of Substance

Long ago in Japan there was a distinguished physician named Nawa Kakei. One day as he was returning home from a journey to Edo, a messenger came to inform him that a wealthy townsman had fallen ill, and to ask if he would please come examine him. "He is the richest man in these parts," added the messenger; "so be sure to diagnose him with even more care than you ordinarily would."

Kakei's good humor vanished. "When you first asked me to look at him, I was prepared to do so right away," he said, "but I no longer have the slightest inclination to do so. Please convey my regrets to the patient."

"But why?"

"It's simple. I was prepared to offer my services to a sick man, but now you tell me that because he is rich, I am to examine him with special care. I have diagnosed many a sick man, but never once have I diagnosed a man's money."

The messenger could not help but admire this stand, and took his leave after offering apologies. What made Kakei great was not his medical proficiency alone, but a character impervious to the claims of wealth and power. Herein lay the secret of the benevolent art he practiced.

24.

Parents Are Mirrored in Their Children

Jacques was an honest man living in the backwoods of France. He was so poor that he was unable to repay the money he owed his neighbor. Out of necessity, he asked his neighbor to accept as payment a half-dozen chickens he had raised.

The following day, after Jacques and his wife left home to work in the fields, the hens returned to their old nests and each laid an egg. Seven-year-old Philippe, the couple's son, saw this and excitedly started to put the eggs in a basket so his mother could cook them later. Then it hit him: since the hens did not belong to his family anymore, the eggs, too, must belong to the neighbor instead.

Straightaway, the little boy took the eggs next door. Impressed, the neighbor asked, "Did your father or mother send you here, Philippe?"

"No, they're out working in the fields," replied the lad, "but I'm sure they'd tell me to bring you the eggs as soon as they got home."

Moved by such integrity, the neighbor gave Philippe two hens as a reward. The boy grew up to become a great statesman.

Honest actions bring success.

In a certain city, children six and under could ride the local train for free. One day a young mother came on board with her small daughter, aged about seven. A passenger seated across the way said, "Oh, what a sweet little girl. How old are you, dear?"

The child turned to her mother and said, "Mommy, which one should I tell her—how old I am at home, or how old I am when we take the train?"

The mother turned crimson. By teaching her child to lie about her age to save a paltry train fare, she was inflicting damage on an innocent soul.

It is senseless for a mother crab to tell her babies to walk forward when she herself walks sideways.

Unless the needle sews straight, the thread will wind up crooked.

Children's behavior reflects the image of their parents, for good or for ill. However poverty-stricken parents may be, they must rise above their hardships and live with honesty and courage. They must do so for their own sake and for the sake of their precious children.

25

Reading in the Dark

Horin's Love of Books

Horin (1693–1741) was a highly learned and gifted Shin Buddhist priest. When he was seventeen, he served as a temple acolyte. One evening the temple night watchman was making his rounds when he was startled to come across someone sitting in the darkness behind the Lecture Hall, reading avidly.

"Who's there?" he called out.

"It's me, Horin," came the answer.

"How can you read in the dark?"

The youth looked up at his questioner—and when he looked back down at the page, found he could no longer make out the words. Until that moment he had been so absorbed that he was able to read in the dark.

Another time, a friend invited him to join in a group going swimming. Without getting up, Horin said, "Wait a minute, I want to finish reading this." The friend waited and waited, but Horin showed no sign of stopping.

"Come on!" his friend said finally.

"Go on ahead of me," said Horin. "I'll be along. This is so interesting I can't put it down."

"Well, wear this hat when you come," said his friend, and stuck it on his head sideways.

Evening came, but Horin never showed up. When the others came trooping back, they found him still sitting with the hat on sideways, immersed in his book.

The waterwheel,
keeps going—
no time to freeze.

26

Kindness Benefits Oneself as Well as Others

Watanabe Kazan's Rules for Business

A merchant once asked the famous thinker Watanabe Kazan (1793–1841) the secrets of business success. Watanabe obligingly came up with the following rules:

1. Get up before your servants.
2. Treat a small spender with greater consideration than a big spender.
3. When a customer returns an item he is displeased with, treat him with even greater courtesy than when he bought it.
4. The more you prosper, the more frugal you should be.
5. Write down every cent you spend on yourself.

6. Don't forget the determination of your first business venture.
7. When a competitor opens up in the neighborhood, develop cordial relations with him and encourage one another warmly.
8. When you open a branch store, lay in food for three years.

In all ages, "early to bed and early to rise" has been a secret of success.

There is a tendency to make much of rich people and slight the poor, but it is imperative to look after the needs of the poor and take their side. Likewise, however inconvenient it may be to do so, it is important to sympathize with others and deal with them courteously.

The more others respect and admire you, the more circumspect you need to be in words and deeds.

Everything in this world, even a scrap of paper, exists as a means of attaining the purpose of life and must be treated with respect.

If you are fortunate enough to enjoy great success, you should never forget the spirit of the beginner, and not grow indolent and arrogant.

When a rival comes along, he should be appreciated as someone who has appeared to spur you on to greater efforts and self-improvement.

Kindness does not only benefit others. It benefits you yourself as well. Spare no effort to see that others live in perfect contentment.

27.

The Color of Flames

The Master Painter and the Veteran Firefighter

The Japanese artist Tsukioka Yoshitoshi (1839–92) established a school of ukiyoe (a type of Japanese woodblock printing) that combined traditional techniques with those of Western art. Once he rushed off to the scene of a great fire to sketch the swirling flames. A few days later, a firefighter he knew well came by, and Yoshitoshi showed him the sketch.

"I did this of the big fire the other day. I'd like your expert opinion. Is there anything wrong in my drawing?"

The sketch was masterfully done. Everything from the leaping flames to the roiling clouds of black smoke and people's horrified screams was realistically and powerfully portrayed. The firefighter studied it awhile in silence before commenting.

"As a matter of fact, I happened to be away that night, so I didn't see the fire myself. Judging from this picture, though, it must have been a hardware store that burned."

Yoshitoshi was amazed. "You're right! I drew this looking at a burning hardware store. But how could you know that when there is nothing here but fire and smoke?"

"I've been a firefighter for many years, so I can tell by the color of the flames whether it's wood or metal that is burning. The flames in this picture of yours are definitely the color of burning metal."

Yoshitoshi was even more impressed. "The trained eye is truly a formidable thing. Your ability to distinguish between different colors of flames is of enormous interest to me."

While the firefighter's ability deserves praise, Yoshitoshi's painting, too, was clearly the work of a master. Learning the hidden mysteries of any field leads to remarkable discoveries.

28

Someone's Lot Today Will Be Mine Tomorrow

The Unjust Law of Benares

Long ago, the Indian kingdom of Benares had an abominable law. When a man reached sixty years of age, his children had to give him a mat on which to sit day and night, guarding the gate of the home.

In this kingdom lived a man whose wife died young, leaving him with two small sons to raise. He brought them up by himself in extreme poverty. Finally he reached the age of sixty. The older son, who acted as though he had raised himself, told his brother, "Find a mat and give it to Father, so he can sit by the gate from now on."

The younger brother, who was devoted to their father, racked his brain. Finally he fetched a mat from the storeroom and cut it in half. Choking back tears, he handed half of the mat to the old man and said, "Father, I am very sorry, but it is my brother's order. Starting today, you must sit on this mat and watch over the gate."

Puzzled, his brother asked, "Why didn't you give him the whole mat?"

"We have only one," came the reply. "If I give it all to Father now, that will mean trouble down the road when we need another mat, won't it?"

"Why would we need another mat?" asked the older brother, more mystified than ever. "Who would use it?"

"No one stays young forever. The other half is for you."

"For me? Why?"

"When you turn sixty, won't your children be distressed if there is no mat for you?"

The older brother realized with a shock that someday his own children would force the same ignominy on him. Awakened to the injustice of the perfidious law, he stood up with his younger brother to fight it, and together they succeeded in having it struck from the books.

The lot of someone else today will be my lot tomorrow. Shifts and changes are inevitable in life. But often we are so filled with self-importance that we find it difficult to perceive the stark reality of our inevitable end.

29

Cats All Steal Fish

A man came home to find his wife standing in the kitchen with a stick in her hand, raised threateningly in the air.

"Hey, what's going on?" he asked.

"Hi," she said. "I'm furious."

"What's wrong?"

"Today I bought some of your favorite fish for dinner, and it cost a pretty penny, too. I laid it on the carving board and then turned around to adjust the fire on the stove. The second my back was turned, that cat of ours jumped up, grabbed the fish, and ran off. I called and called, but it just glared at me and growled. I'm so mad, I don't know what to do."

"I see. Well, let's sort out what happened. Did the cat know that it was my favorite fish, or that it cost a pretty penny?"

"Of course not. It's only a cat."

"Is ours the only cat who steals fish?"

"No, they're all the same."

"What about a cook who lets a cat get the better of her? Would you say she's smart or otherwise? I'm afraid if Buddha judged this case, you, the plaintiff, would end up paying all the court costs."

"All right, never mind. I won't hit the cat."

"No, by all means, go right ahead and deliver a beating."

"But the cat's not to blame."

"Who is?"

"Me."

"Then hit yourself with the stick."

Cats have been stealing fish since the beginning of time.

We are tormented with anger because we are convinced we are right.

30

On Mastering an Art

Whatever the art, it cannot be mastered unless the pupil is thrown into a ravine and made to crawl back up again and again. "Kindness" results in superficial understanding.

31

Count to Ten When Angry

Or You May Find Yourself Weeping Alone

A zoo hippopotamus became pregnant. Her keepers waited eagerly for the birth, but when the time came, to their great disappointment the baby hippo was stillborn. In searching for the reason, they found that when the mother was transferred to a different room during her pregnancy, she had for some reason gone berserk with anger, and this episode had resulted in the death of the fetus. I remember being shocked on reading this account of needless tragedy in the newspaper. Anger, it seems, releases toxins into the system that can destroy physical health.

The effects of anger on humans are just as disastrous. One often hears accounts of street quarrels that turn into fights in which someone collapses in rage before ever landing a blow. And there is a famous story of an eminent priest who spent forty years reciting the Lotus Sutra, only for all the merit so painstakingly acquired to be lost in a moment's angry outburst.

When blood rushes to the head in a fit of anger, we may say and do things we would never dream of ordinarily—and as a result find ourselves standing alone in a charred wasteland, weeping bitter tears. But if in the moment of anger we take a second to think why we are outraged, what it is that so upsets us, our indignation often melts away.

If you have been attacked even though you are in the right, there is no need to blame your attacker. Eventually he is bound to come round and beg your forgiveness. No one is a match for the truth. If you discover that you are in error, then follow the proverb, "It's never too late to mend." Take swift steps to correct the matter and improve yourself. To defend yourself furiously even though you are wrong is the height of folly.

The aftermath of anger is dreary emptiness. So when you get angry, count to ten, and when someone else gets angry, steer clear of him or her. This is the wise counsel of ancients.

32

The Lesson of the Red Camellia

One night a man in the prime of life got up to go to the bathroom. On the way, he spat into the garden. To his horror, his sputum was bright red, a telltale sign of tuberculosis. His legs turned to jelly and he sank to the floor.

When the man didn't come back to bed, his wife grew concerned and went looking for him. She laid a hand on his forehead and found he had a raging fever. The household was soon in an uproar, and they sent for a doctor. Meanwhile the man told his wife what had happened, and she went out to the garden to see for herself. She discovered that he'd spat onto the fallen petal of a scarlet camellia. When she told him this, his fever magically disappeared, and the next morning, he set off for work as usual. If he hadn't found out the truth, he could have made himself truly sick.

There is no need to live in fear of what may come. Change is only natural: the earth itself has day and night, the moon waxes and wanes in the sky, the ocean has its high tide and low. In our lives, too, we experience both fat and lean. When you are at a low point, just wait, for "this too shall pass." When you are at rock bottom, you are undergoing a test. Think of it as Buddha's way of training you so that in time he can give you something better than you have ever known.

A hothouse flower does not smell so sweet as one exposed to wind and cold.

Rain and sunshine are equally good. Anyone who can't appreciate this is of little substance. It is essential to open the eyes of the soul.

33

A Good Wife; a Bad Wife

Paying Attention to Feelings

A man working in an office was shocked when B, a colleague he secretly looked down on, received a promotion ahead of him. When he ran into B, he clapped him on the shoulder and offered hearty congratulations, swallowing his disappointment and forcing himself to act as if nothing was wrong.

All those who had been passed over got together after work to celebrate B's promotion, as if it were the most natural thing in the world. None of them wanted the rest to know how keenly they felt the blow. A man dares not acknowledge humiliation even to himself, but holds his emotions in check.

There is something sad about the price exacted by the male ego.

Worn out after the party, the man faced yet a steeper hurdle. When he came home, his wife was waiting for him.

"Out drinking again, I see."

"Yes. B got a promotion today."

"And you gave a party in his honor?" The man's wife pressed him for details. Then she exclaimed, "You're awfully calm for someone who was skipped over for a promotion!"

"We can't all be promoted at once. Somebody's got to be first."

"Then it should have been you."

"No, B's the man for the job. Anyway, I think I'll take a bath and hit the hay."

"You don't have an ounce of pride, do you?"

The woman had no inkling of her husband's hidden pain, of the effort it cost him to feign indifference to the snub. Nor did she make any attempt to put herself in his shoes. A wise wife would have understood without being told, and let the matter drop. A bad wife fails to catch on to her husband's true feelings in such a case, and needles him unmercifully. No wife should trample her husband's feelings underfoot.

34.

The Poppy Seed and a Mother's Search

During Śākyamuni's time on earth, there was a beautiful woman who married and gave birth to a perfect baby boy. She was a devoted mother, but one day her child sickened and died. In a paroxysm of grief she clasped the tiny body to her breast and went around the village where she lived, asking if anyone could bring her son back to life. All who saw her were moved to tears. Finally, not knowing what else to do, they directed her to the place where Śākyamuni lived. Straightaway she went to see him and begged him in tears to restore her child to life.

The Buddha responded gently, "I understand how you feel. If you want your beloved child to return to life, you must do as I say. Go to town and bring me a poppy seed from a house where no one has yet died. As soon as you do that, I will bring him to life."

Overjoyed, the woman hurried to town. But wherever she went, she was turned away. "My father died last year," said one person. "I lost my husband this year," said another. "My child died just the other day," said someone else. Every house had poppy seeds, but no house was free of death. Still the grieving mother wouldn't give up, but kept running around frantically in search of a house where no one had ever died. Finally it grew dark. Exhausted, she dragged herself back to Śākyamuni.

"Couldn't you get a poppy seed?" he asked.

"No, for death had come to every house I visited. I finally understood that my child, too, is dead."

"That's right. Everyone dies. That fact is clear, yet people can't see it."

"Yes," said the woman, "I was blind. If you hadn't made me go through this, I would never have understood. Please tell me how someone as foolish as I am can be saved."

She listened intently to the Buddha's words from then on.

35

Treat High and Low Alike

Bismarck: "I Too Am a Shoemaker"

German Chancellor Otto von Bismarck (1815–98) once went deep into the countryside to see some land he had purchased. The arrival of a train there was an event, and people would gather round to see who had come. Anyone out of the ordinary soon became the talk of the town.

The village shoemaker, a particularly curious fellow who liked to spread news, took quick note of the tall and powerfully built Bismarck and watched as he stepped onto the platform, seated himself on a bench, and lit a cigar. "What an extraordinary man!" thought the shoemaker, and respectfully approached the mysterious visitor to see what he could find out.

"Pardon me, sir," he said, "but have you come from Berlin?"

"That's right."

"You are a man of fine build. What do you do?"

"What do you do?" countered Bismarck.

"I am a poor country shoemaker."

"I too am a shoemaker."

The two men continued their conversation until a uniformed man came up and said deferentially, "Sire, your carriage is ready." The shoemaker was stunned. Realizing he had been addressing a man of high station, he humbly apologized for his affrontery.

Bismarck replied affably, "Not at all. If you should ever come to Berlin, please stop by my factory. The address is 76 Wilhelm Street."

The villager never dreamed that he had been speaking to Bismarck. The "blood and iron" chancellor showed himself to be a genial man of the people, one who treated all alike, high and low.

36

On Seed-Planting

Don't worry about when the seeds will sprout. Just plant them. The world is full of people who spend all their time thinking about the crop they'll reap, without ever planting anything.

37

The Greater the Purpose …

The Squirrel and the Lake

This is a story about Śākyamuni Buddha in one of his previous lives.

Long ago, a rich young man who had become deeply aware of life's impermanence left his ornate palace to become a mountain ascetic. After some time, he saw a squirrel beside a lake dipping its tail repeatedly in and out of the water. Finding this behavior strange, he asked the squirrel what it was doing.

"I'm emptying the lake with my tail," came the surprising reply.

"You think that by removing water drop by drop with your little tail you can empty this enormous lake? It could take centuries!"

"That's right," replied the squirrel. "Even so, I have no intention of giving up after a mere five or six years. However long it takes, I'm determined to keep on until my fixed desire is achieved."

Inspired by the squirrel's resolution, the young man said to himself, "I too have a great desire, one no less grand than the squirrel's. However many years it takes, I must not lose heart until my hoped-for end is achieved." He kept on with his training, and finally achieved buddhahood.

The squirrel was Śakro devānām indraḥ, the protector of those who are striving to attain enlightenment. The young man, discouraged by his failure to achieve buddhahood, had been toying with the idea of giving up and returning to his father's palace. Śakro devānām indraḥ took the form of a squirrel to encourage him and make him see that without a resolve of steel, he could never achieve his purpose.

The greater the purpose you are trying to achieve, the more important it is to remember that nothing can be achieved without firm determination. At the same time, it often happens that in their haste, people overreach themselves, become exhausted, and lose their way—just the opposite of what they meant to do. In all things, it is wise to make haste slowly. The more important your ultimate goal, the more crucial it is to watch where you are going and move forward with caution, step by step.

38

If You Are Caught Up in the Here and Now, You Lose Sight of the Future

The Wisdom of Napoleon

Napoleon returned home in triumph after successive victories over Italy and Austria. The people welcomed him in a frenzy of jubilation, with illuminations, parades and banners, torches and bells, and gun salutes.

One of Napoleon's men offered him respectful congratulations: "Sire, it must gratify you to receive such a rousing welcome."

To his surprise, Napoleon answered coolly, "Don't talk nonsense. It is a great mistake to enjoy such a superficial fuss. If circumstances were slightly different, these same people would be clamoring 'To the guillotine!' just as loudly.

Nothing is so unreliable as the welcome of a mass of blind followers."

The great swordsman Chiba Shusaku (1794–1855) went fishing one night with several of his followers. They set out with torches, heading farther and farther to sea in search of fish, until they lost all sense of direction. Which way was the shore?

Shusaku himself grew flustered and had a series of torches lit while he peered in vain into the gloom. As they roamed the sea with mounting panic, the last of the torches burned out. The situation seemed hopeless. But lo and behold, as darkness settled in, there in the distance was the outline of land, looming darker still. The men whooped in relief and joy.

Days later, Shusaku recounted the incident to a fisherman friend of his. The friend said smilingly, "That wasn't like you. You should know that you can't see the shore with torches. Torches are used to light up your immediate surroundings. If you want to see into the distance, they only get in the way. When we want to look far off, we douse them on purpose."

As long as you rely on torches, you cannot make out the distant shore.

If you are caught up in the here and now, you cannot look ahead into the future.

39

The Destructive Power of Speech

Killed Twenty-four Times

A very old woman, over 120 years of age, once had a visitor who commented, "You must have had many rare and interesting experiences over the course of your long lifetime. Will you please share one of those memories with me?"

"I'm sure lots of things did happen, but my memory isn't what it used to be; I'm afraid I have forgotten them all," replied the old woman, shaking her head.

The visitor sympathized, saying that was only natural for someone of her advanced years, but persisted, "Isn't there at least one thing you do remember?"

“Well, if you insist, I’ll tell you. I have painful memories of being killed twenty-four times.” The old woman mumbled these mysterious words half to herself, her wrinkled face settling into a frown. When asked to explain, she began to tell her story bit by bit in a sorrowful tone, pausing frequently.

“During my lifetime, I’ve seen the births of many children, grandchildren, and great-grandchildren. But it is the way of life that death can strike anyone, young or old, and so it sometimes happened that a child or grandchild of mine would predecease me. We’ve had a total of twenty-four funerals in this house. Each time, I overheard people who came to offer their condolences say, ‘If only the old woman had died instead!’ They at least would whisper it in another room out of deference to me, but my grandchildren and great-grandchildren would deliberately say such things to my face. Their words killed me again and again.”

Truly, the mouth is the gateway to misfortune. We will never know how many people we may have injured or killed with our words.

40.

He Who Saves Others Will Be Saved Himself

The Lion and the Mouse

The lion, king of the jungle, was dozing after a heavy meal. As he stretched out his paw, he seized a tiny mouse. The mouse cried desperately: "Oh mighty king lion, please let me go. If you spare me now, I will never forget your kindness. In your moment of need, I'll be sure to repay you."

The lion laughed out loud. "I don't believe I'll ever need help from the likes of you," he said. "I'm full now, so I'll spare your life. Now go!" he said, and roared haughtily. The mouse thanked the lion over and over and left.

Moments later, as the lion was roaming the forest, he fell into a large snare. His legs and neck became entangled in the net, and the harder he struggled, the more tightly the rope choked him. Soon he was hardly able to breathe.

The mouse whose life he had just spared heard what was happening and came running to help. "Oh great king," he said, "I will now save your life." Then he gnawed through the ropes and set the lion free.

Things are not to be measured by inches, for even a tiny mouse may help a mighty lion. As we live embraced with kindness, there is no knowing when we too may receive a great favor. We ourselves must render kindness at all times and spread compassion over all things.

41

The Boatman Who Disobeyed His Lord's Command

True Professionalism

In medieval Japan, a lord sailing through the Seto Inland Sea was scheduled to arrive in Osaka later that day. Though there was not a cloud in the sky, the captain suddenly began ordering his crew to lower the sail and pull into the bay of Takasago. The lord had frequently traveled in this area and was used to the waters of Western Japan. He found this action strange and summoned the captain.

"What is going on here?" he asked severely.

"Sir, I am terribly sorry, but a storm is on the way and we must be cautious. I do not want harm to come upon you, so I decided to delay our voyage."

"You idiot! Look at this weather! There is absolutely no sign of a storm coming! Never mind what you think, set sail immediately!"

Following this tongue-lashing, the captain withdrew in silence. Nonetheless, he headed the ship for the bay at an even faster clip. The lord was infuriated.

"How dare you disobey my orders! If the weather remains the same, I'll have your head."

"Certainly, my lord," the captain answered coolly. "If the weather holds, there could be no better news for you. If I am wrong, I will commit seppuku (ritual suicide by disembowelment) to atone."

Within the hour, the sky clouded over and fierce winds began to blow. Though the ship was in grave danger, the captain led his crew safely through the storm with no loss of life.

After this sterling performance, the captain told his fourteen-year-old son, "The captain of a ship takes no orders from anyone else. He runs his ship as he sees fit, even if he has to sacrifice his own life. Never forget what happened today."

The lord came to admire the captain immensely and sang his praises.

The person who can assert his will in the face of authority and threats is a true professional. Only true professionals can accomplish great things.

42

Detecting Fakes

Carrying Out One's Mission

Charles M. Schwab (1862–1939), the first president of the United States Steel Corporation, once had to make a quick trip to his office after hours. When he came to the gate, the guard refused to admit him. "No one is allowed in at this hour."

"But I'm Schwab, the company president."

"I don't know what the company president looks like, so I'm sorry, sir, but unless you've got some I.D. I can't let you in."

Schwab duly presented some identification, and so was able to take care of his errand. The following day, the guard received a summons to the president's office. He went fearing a dressing-down, but instead received a promotion directly from Schwab himself.

Once when Winston Churchill was prime minister, he was tearing along in great haste when his car came to an intersection with a red light. Traffic was not heavy, so Churchill ordered his driver, "Never mind! Run the light!"

As the car started across the intersection, a traffic policeman darted out and ordered it back.

"I'm Churchill! I'm in a hurry."

The policeman gave him a hard look and said, "Prime Minister Churchill would never commit a traffic violation. I believe you are a fake. Get back where you belong."

Deflated, Churchill said meekly, "Very well. You're right, I'm a fake." He ordered his driver to back up.

A few days later, Churchill sought to have the traffic policeman promoted, but the policeman demurred. "I did nothing to deserve a promotion."

"Yes, you did," replied the prime minister. "You identified me as an imposter. I'm sure you have the same ability where criminals are concerned. This promotion is a reward for your powers of discernment."

43

Rewarding the Unfilial Son

An Approach to Good and Bad

A samurai was on a journey. His retainer fell behind, so he paused to wait for him. At last the retainer came rushing up, out of breath.

"What were you doing?" asked the samurai.

"My straw sandals broke, so I was fixing them."

"Who gave you the straw?"

"No one. I took it from some rice plants laid out to dry by the side of the road."

"Did you ask permission first?"

"No," said the retainer. "Nobody would care about a stalk or two of rice straw. Everybody does it, anyway."

"You fool," said the samurai. "I won't put up with such an attitude. Everyone else may allow it, but I will not. Go back and ask the owner's pardon."

The samurai well knew that those two excuses—"Everyone does it" and "It's so small it doesn't matter"—are always on the devil's tongue.

Lord Tokugawa Mitsukuni (1628–1700) was on a tour of inspection. A local man known for abusing his mother heard that the lord would reward anyone who demonstrated uncommon filial respect. Eager to receive a prize, he hoisted his aged mother on his back and joined the parade to welcome the distinguished visitor.

Mitsukuni caught sight of the man carrying his mother and ordered an attendant to reward him.

"Surely you don't mean it, sir," said the attendant. "The fellow is known for the atrocious way he treats his mother most of the time. He's only here today with her on his back to try to fool you into giving him something."

Mitsukuni listened thoughtfully and then said, "What difference does it make? Even if he's only making a small gesture, and even if it's only for today, that's all right. The important thing is, at least this one time he has accorded her proper respect. Give him a rich reward."

He who comes in contact with red dye is stained red. We are shaped by the people who surround us. He who associates with good people will find himself becoming good. Do good, even if it is only an act of imitation.

44

On Self-Reflection

Everyone makes mistakes. Whether we put our mistakes to use depends on how deeply we reflect on our actions. It is desirable to reflect until the tears come.

45

The Importance of Quick-Wittedness

The Salesman and the Housewife

A salesman rang the doorbell and asked to speak to the lady of the house. A woman grudgingly appeared and asked him haughtily, "What do you want?"

"Is the lady of the house at home?"

Looking even more displeased, the woman said curtly, "I am the lady of the house. What is it?"

"Oh, I'm so sorry. I didn't realize." The salesman bowed his head apologetically as he pulled out a catalog. "The truth is, you're so young and pretty that I mistook you for the daughter. Forgive me."

People are so conceited that they fall even for obvious flattery. The woman's attitude changed as easily as a child forgets its tears, like a clear sky after a drizzle.

"Oh, what a flatterer!" she simpered. "And what do you have there? I wonder if there's anything I need. Could I see it?"

The salesman's success was due to his shrewd understanding of human nature.

The following story also illustrates the importance of quick-wittedness.

One night, someone collided with the manager of a store as he came around the corner. Since the manager always scolded his clerks for their blunders, from force of habit he barked, "Fool!" Then, seeing to his consternation that the other person was his boss, the company president, he swiftly added with a bow, "… am I not? Good night, sir."

After this dazzling display of quick-wittedness, the president was unable to get angry and went on his way with a chuckle.

Though we must refrain from calling others "fools," it would certainly be nice to have the kind of mind that can react so quickly.

46

Sticking to a Single Path in Life

One night, a mouse fell into a bucket. At first he tried mightily to jump out, but the bucket was deep, the task hopeless. Next he tried to gnaw a hole in the side of the bucket, but the wood proved too hard and too thick for him to gnaw through. Giving up, he moved frantically to another place and tried gnawing there for a while, but the results were the same. Again he gave up and tried a different spot. The stout wood was impervious to his efforts.

After gnawing in vain all night long, toward dawn, worn out in body and spirit, the mouse collapsed and died. If only he had kept gnawing at the same spot the whole time, he might have gnawed all the way through and escaped.

The world is full of people who cannot afford to laugh at the story of the hapless mouse. Failing at one job, they try another and fail again, changing their job over and over. Such people may be called weak-willed; yet weakness is a general human failing.

Sticking to a single path in life is hard to do. It requires a will of steel and ceaseless effort. The more you waver, the more your life's efforts go to waste. Since this is the case, the thing to do is weigh your options carefully to begin with, make a careful decision, and carry it through with firm and unremitting effort. The entrance to a commuter train at rush hour can be so crowded that it seems impossible to squeeze another person on board—yet if you push on through, you'll often find there is plenty of room further in. No one should ever despair because the entrance to his or her chosen career path is clogged.

There is an ancient saying: "The persistent drip wears through stone."

47

The Man Who Had Everything

What Is Happiness?

American Wallace H. Carothers (1896–1937) invented nylon, a revolutionary new textile that was soon used to produce stockings of dramatic resiliency. His employers at DuPont rewarded their brilliant chemist with exceptional treatment. For as long as he lived, wherever he traveled and whatever five-star restaurant he chose to eat in, the company agreed to shoulder the cost. Undoubtedly they were happy to do this if it kept their star employee from being wooed away by other firms. If he became disgruntled and leaked the secret of nylon manufacture to a competitor, they would suffer a devastating loss. The cost of a lifetime of travel and fine dining must have seemed a small price to pay.

Despite this promise of a life of ease, Carothers killed himself at the young age of forty-one.

In a tropical country, an American scolded a native who spent all his time napping under a palm tree. "Stop being so lazy!" he lectured him sternly. "Why don't you get a job and make yourself some money?"

"What would I do with money?"

"Save it in the bank and before you know it, you'll have a big pile."

"What would I do with a pile of money?"

"Build a fine house for yourself. Then if you made more money, you could have a villa."

"What would I do with a villa?"

"You could go out in the garden and nap under a palm tree."

"I already am napping under a palm tree."

What is human happiness? The American in the story above expounds the view promoted by humanity in general. Carothers' story clearly demonstrates the futility of this philosophy.

48

Perseverance Is Greater than Proficiency

Cūḍa-panthaka's Long Years of Cleaning

Cūḍa-panthaka, one of Śākyamuni's most famous disciples, was dull by birth, unable to remember even his own name. One day Śākyamuni found him crying and asked him kindly, "Why are you so sad?"

Weeping bitterly, Cūḍa-panthaka lamented, "Why was I born stupid?"

"Cheer up," said Śākyamuni. "You are aware of your foolishness, but there are many fools who think themselves wise. Being aware of one's stupidity is next to enlightenment." He handed Cūḍa-panthaka a broom and instructed him to say while he worked, "I sweep the dust away. I wash the dirt away."

Cūḍa-panthaka tried desperately to remember those sacred phrases from the Buddha, but whenever he remembered one, he forgot the other. Even so, he kept at his chore for twenty years.

Once during those twenty years, Śākyamuni complimented Cūḍa-panthaka on his determination. "No matter how many years you keep sweeping, you grow no better at it, and yet that does not cause you to give up. As important as making progress is, persevering in the same endeavor is even more important. It is an admirable trait—one that I do not see in my other disciples."

In time Cūḍa-panthaka realized that dust and dirt accumulated not only where he thought they would, but in places he least expected. He thought, "I knew I was stupid, but there's no knowing how much more of my stupidity exists in places I don't even notice."

In the end Cūḍa-panthaka attained the enlightenment of an arhat, a very high stage. Besides encountering a great teacher and true teachings, it was his long years of effort and perseverance that crowned him with success.

49.

Even If You Become Rich, Never Forget Your Former Poverty

Yataro Iwasaki and His Mother

Yataro Iwasaki (1834–85), the Japanese entrepreneur and founder of the Mitsubishi Group, was a man of deep integrity and a financial giant of his times. Even so, when he visited the homes of government ministers and other eminences he always wore straw sandals. When asked why, he would answer, "It's what my mother taught me."

Even after Yataro's rise to national prominence, his mother continued to weave straw sandals for him to wear. She would hand them to him and say, "Even if you have become rich, you must never forget your former poverty and become proud."

Once a man called at the home of an American magnate to ask for a charitable contribution. When he arrived, he overheard him scolding a servant: "All you need is a little bit. Why did you use so much?" Wondering what it was that the servant had used too much of, he listened closely and found it was glue. "A man that stingy isn't likely to make a contribution," he thought glumly, but he went ahead and made his pitch. His host surprised him with a generous donation of five hundred dollars on the spot.

Surprised at the discrepancy, the man asked about the glue incident and was told, "I do my best to waste nothing, not even a bit of glue. That is why I have money to donate to your cause."

Use things wastefully and you are sure to suffer privation in the end. All things exist to help us achieve the purpose of human life, so nothing, however small, must be treated with disrespect.

50

Don't Judge People by Appearance

Ikkyu and the Guard

A rich man in Kyoto invited the famous Zen monk Ikkyu (1394–1481) to hold a Buddhist service at his home. The day before, Ikkyu happened to pass the man's gate, so he decided to stop by. The guard yelled at him sternly: "All right, you beggar priest! If you're here to beg, go around to the back!"

"No, I'm here to speak to the master of the house."

"Ha. What makes you think he'd speak to the likes of you?" The guard based his judgment on the shabby vestments Ikkyu was wearing.

"It's your job to announce visitors, isn't it? Tell him there's someone here to see him."

"Who do you think you are, talking to me that way?" The guard chased Ikkyu away in a fury.

The following day Ikkyu came by with his disciples, dressed in his formal purple robe, and presented himself at the front gate. This time the guard bowed his head reverently and let him right in.

When Ikkyu entered the drawing room, he said to his host with a grin, "Well, sir, I had quite a reception here yesterday."

"Oh, did you come by yesterday?"

"Yes, I had a little business to take care of. But when I said I wanted to see you, the guard called me a beggar priest and chased me away."

"Dear me. I had no idea. I apologize sincerely for his rude behavior. But why did you not tell him your name?"

As the master prostrated himself in abject apology, Ikkyu cast aside his purple vestment. "I myself am of no value whatever. It is this purple vestment that is valuable, so have it read the sutra."

He left the robe behind and went home.

Never judge people by appearance. The value of a human being cannot be told from the outside.

51

Start with the Third Floor!

Ignorance of the Law of Causality

A foolish man was invited to the house-warming party for his friend's brand-new three-story house. He was amazed at the scale of the building, for three-story structures were a rarity there. His friend boasted of the view from the third floor, and the man himself was amazed when he saw it. He decided that he, too, would build such a house, and went straight off to the village carpenter.

"Build me a three-story house right away," he instructed. Since he had an inheritance from his father, he was the richest man in the village. Money was no object.

Being hasty as well as foolish, one day soon afterward he went to see how his house was coming along, expecting it to be nearly finished. He found a large crew of men at work on the foundation, digging deep into the ground. As soon as he realized what they were doing, he called them together and began to scold.

"What's going on? I asked for a three-story building with a view, and here you are digging a hole in the ground!"

The construction foreman replied, "Well, sir, a good foundation is important, because otherwise the third floor might end up off-kilter. When we finish this, we'll move on to the first floor, then the second—"

The foolish man said indignantly, "Did I ask you to build a first floor or a second floor? No! All I want is the third floor! So get busy and build it!"

On hearing this, the carpenters exchanged looks and burst out laughing.

Too many people seek only a third floor with a fine view, paying no attention to the foundation needed to build it, and then moan and carry on when they can't have it.

52

On Asking Favors

It's better to ask for something that costs a little to give than something that can be given painlessly. When someone asks if there's anything you want, be sure to show inordinate pleasure. Saying "No thanks, I don't need anything" results in a net loss for all.

53

Those Who Lack Compassion

Kindness Tested

One day, Śākyamuni went out disguised as a beggar. He knocked on the door of a house and asked for a bowl of rice.

"I cook only enough for my husband and myself," said the housewife coldly.

"Then could you offer me a cup of tea?"

"Tea is too good for a beggar. Water should be good enough."

"I feel so weak I can hardly move. Will you please fetch me some water?"

"Some nerve … a beggar ordering people around! There's plenty of water in the river in front of the house, so go over there and drink to your heart's content."

Suddenly Śākyamuni revealed himself and said, "What a merciless person you are! Had you offered me a bowl of rice, I would have given you this iron bowl full of gold. Had you offered me a cup of tea, I would have given it to you full of silver, and had you offered me water, I would have given it to you full of tin. But you have no kindness. No happiness will ever come to you as you are."

"Oh, Śākyamuni, is it you? Here, please accept an offering."

"I cannot. Charity that expects something in return is mixed with poison. I will not accept anything from you." With this, Śākyamuni turned and left.

When the woman's husband came home, she told him the whole story. "You're so stupid," he said. "Why didn't you offer him the bowl of rice in the first place? Then you could have gotten a bowlful of gold in exchange."

"Believe me, if I'd known that, I'd have given him ten bowls of rice."

"All right, I'll go after him and give him some rice in exchange for gold," said the husband, and took off after Śākyamuni.

Just as his strength was giving out, he came to a fork in the road. A beggar was crouched by the roadside.

"Hey, beggar," said the husband. "Did Śākyamuni pass by here?"

"That I do not know, sir, but ... I'm so famished I cannot move. Won't you please give me something to eat?"

"I didn't come here to feed you. I came for gold."

At that moment, Śākyamuni revealed himself and said: "The husband is no better than the wife. Those who lack compassion will receive no happiness."

"Ah, so you were Śākyamuni all along? It's you I came here to give this to."

"No. Offerings made for the sake of honor and profit are poisoned. I shall not accept them." With this solemn reply, Śākyamuni went on his way.

54.

The Shaman Who Ate Cow Dung

Ignorance Leads to Superstition

Once there was a couple blessed with three children, all of them girls. They were eager for a son as well. The wife became pregnant, but her husband told her, "It's probably another girl." Just as she was feeling pessimistic about her chances of giving birth to a boy, a man came calling and asked her which she thought it would be, a girl or a boy.

"I have no idea," she said.

"Which are you hoping for?" he persisted.

"I'd love to have a boy this time," she said honestly.

"Well, I have divine power" said the man, "and I am sorry to say that it is another girl."

Interested despite herself, she asked, "How do you know?"

"I have special power. But if you pray, there is still time to change the sex of the child. If you like, I will offer prayers on your behalf."

"But … that must be expensive."

"I seek only to help others; money is nothing to me. But each prayer must be accompanied by a thank offering of five thousand yen. Four or five prayers should do it."

The wife was only half convinced, but the amount of money was not great, and she knew how thrilled her husband would be with a son. And so, without telling anyone, she asked the shaman to perform the series of prayers.

Finally the last day came. As usual, the husband set off for work, and then the shaman came by. But today the husband forgot something and retraced his steps, only to find a strange man laying strips of paper on his wife's belly and chanting a spell with all his might. After listening silently to his wife's abashed explanation, the man bowed to the shaman and excused himself. He went out and bought some bean-jam buns, removed the bean-jam, and replaced it with cow dung. When he came back, he invited the shaman to help himself.

The shaman had feared a commotion, but at this display of hospitality he relaxed and bit off a big mouthful. When he realized that he had been made to eat cow dung, he sputtered with indignation.

The man and his wife both laughed. "Looks like you don't have power to see beneath the outer layer of a bun!" said the husband.

The shaman fled, shamefaced.

The heart of darkness is ever prey to silly superstitions.

55

First, Master the Basics

A youth came to the home of a famous Italian master to beg for voice instruction, only to be curtly refused. "Give it up," said the master. "The way of a musician is hard." Earnestly, the youth replied, "I will endure any suffering. Please teach me." On condition that he never utter a word of complaint, however difficult his life became, the musician finally consented to take him on.

That very day the youth moved in and commenced to study voice in between managing all the household cooking, cleaning, and laundry. For the entire first year, he practiced nothing but scales. The second year was more of the same. He hoped that in the third year he might be allowed to work on something else, but again it was scales, scales, and more scales.

When the fourth year ended the same way, the youth finally expressed dissatisfaction. "Sir, could you possibly teach me something else?" The master dismissed the words with a sharp rebuke.

In his fifth year, the student learned the chromatic scale and how to sing sotto voce. At the end of the year, the master told him, "You may go now. I have no more to teach you. Now you can sing in front of anyone without fear."

The youth's name was Gaetano Majorano (1710–83). Under the stage name Caffarelli he went on to become the greatest Italian opera singer of the eighteenth century.

It's wrong to look down on "mere" scales and exercises. The master poured his soul into teaching them to the prodigy for five years precisely because he knew that once he had mastered the basics, he would be able to sing any music, however difficult.

In any endeavor, mastering the basics is essential.

56

Savoring Jingoro's Sculpture

Skill and Wisdom

One of the greatest sculptors of all time was Hidari ("Left-Handed") Jingoro, who carved the famous "Sleeping Cat" at the Toshogu Shrine in Nikko, the "Ascending Dragon" at Ueno's Kan'eiji temple, and many other famous works. His contemporary Kikuchi Togoro was ranked his equal in those days.

Competing for top honors is only natural. In baseball, chess, and many other fields, spectators enjoy watching competitions and rooting for their favorite team or player. Gradually, competition between factions favoring each of the two artists heated to fever pitch. People began to clamor for the situation to be resolved: "Two sculptors can't both be the best! Let's settle it once and for all."

When the matter came to the attention of the shogun, he summoned the two men and said, "Let us see which of you is the greater. Carve me a mouse on the spot."

The two sculptors set straight to work and finished in no time. Both carvings were so lifelike that they seemed about to squeak and run off. It was impossible to choose between them. The shogun was stumped, until a retainer with a quick mind whispered in his ear, "Cats are experts on mice. Why not let a cat do the deciding?"

The shogun gave a nod of approval. Without further ado, the two carved mice were set in different places in the room, and a cat was released to go after them. It went straight to Togoro's mouse. Everyone thought the contest was over, but in the next moment the cat dropped that one, sprang upon Jingoro's mouse instead, and carried it off in its mouth. The rafters rang with applause and shouts of admiration for the masterful achievement.

Togoro's mouse was carved out of wood, Jingoro's out of *katsuobushi*—a dried fish product sold in woodlike blocks. Skill is not the only mark of a true master. The wisdom to adapt to circumstances is also required.

57

Suffering Insults and Persecution

A Necessary Sacrifice

As dusk came on, a lantern-lit stagecoach made its way along a country road in the old West. Inside, the seats were nearly full, the atmosphere harmonious. As the stagecoach approached a steep and thickly overgrown section of mountain road, uneasy whispers arose among the passengers.

"This area is full of gangs," said one.

"Lots of stagecoaches are ambushed," said another. "I wonder if we're safe."

"This is just the sort of lonely area where it might happen," said someone else.

A young man turned trembling to the dignified gentleman sitting next to him. "Is it true? I'm carrying three thousand dollars that I earned with my sweat and blood. It means my very life. What'll I do?"

The gentleman nodded and said, "I have an idea. Hide it in your boot. They'll never look there."

The young man quickly followed this advice, and not a moment too soon. Just then the stagecoach came under attack. A gang of robbers stormed aboard and began methodically stripping passengers of their valuables. All at once the gentleman cried out, "This fellow is carrying a fortune in his boot!"

Overjoyed at these unexpectedly rich spoils, the brigands took off, not bothering with anyone else. The stagecoach continued on its way, none the worse for the attack, but now all the passengers joined in heaping abuse on the betrayer. The young man accused him wildly of being in league with the robbers. The atmosphere turned ugly.

Through it all, the gentleman merely repeated calmly, "I'm sorry, truly sorry. Just bear with me a little longer."

When the stagecoach pulled into town, the young man's patience wore out and he started to collar the gentleman.

"I'm sorry," repeated the older man. "The truth is, I myself am carrying one hundred thousand dollars. Your three thousand was a great deal of money, but letting it go saved my hundred thousand. Please accept ten thousand dollars as a token of my gratitude. I hope you will forgive me."

On learning the truth, the young man was thoroughly chastened. He offered sincere apologies and thanks to his benefactor.

It is well to realize that sometimes in life it is necessary to disappoint others for a time, and suffer insults and persecution, in order to accomplish a greater purpose.

58

On Living Each Day

Unless you progress a step or a half-step more than yesterday, you haven't really lived today.

59

Do Good Regardless

The Stone in the Center of Town

A king once slipped out of his castle in the middle of the night when nobody was looking and laid a great stone in the center of town. In the morning, a drunken soldier tripped over the stone, fell, and hit his head. "Who put this blasted stone here?" he snarled. "I'd like to teach the damn fool a lesson." Cursing, he went on his way.

Soon a gentleman on horseback came by and just missed running into the stone. He came to a stop and said, "Whew, that was close! I could have been killed. What a dirty trick to play!" Muttering, he trotted on.

After another interval, a farmer came by, pulling his wagon. "What's this?" he cried. "Somebody put a big stone here. It's dangerous and blocks the way." Grumbling, he gave the stone a kick and went on by.

None of them thought to remove the stone.

A month later, the king assembled the people in the town square and admonished them. "I am the one who put the stone here," he said. "But none of you made any attempt to remove it for the public good. That is a sign that my reign is flawed. Today I will personally remove the stone."

When he did so, underneath it was a bag marked, "For Whoever Moves the Stone Out of the Way." It was full of gold and jewels.

Good deeds, even those that go unseen, always bring a reward.

60

Busy People Have the Most Time

The Art of Stealing Moments

A student paid a call on a successful man. "Sir," he said, "I find I am so busy these days that I have no time to study. It's a terrible predicament."

"Don't be ridiculous!" cried his host. "Don't you know that the more you have to do, the more studying you can get done? When you have free time, you probably spend it sleeping. You've got to understand that there's no such thing as special time for studying. Real studying gets done during stolen moments of the day, between other tasks. Anyone who says he's too busy to study is letting his time go to waste. Here's how to achieve superior results: when other people study, keep pace with them, and when they are resting, keep studying then, too. When you're busy, whether you use free moments or waste them is up to you."

"Time flies like an arrow," goes the saying, and indeed the days and months go quickly by. Events of yesterday or today are soon two or three months in the past; half a year or a year goes by in the blink of an eye. Caught up in the daily whirl of mail, telephone calls, and visitors, pressed for time, we let slide what most needs to be done.

The end of life comes quickly, and the all-important question of what happens after death looms large. Let not one moment go to waste.

61

I Saved British Honor

The Pride of a True Gentleman

The distinguished mathematician Dairoku Kikuchi (1855–1917) was educated overseas. While studying at St. John's College in Cambridge, he remained at the head of his class until sidelined by a lengthy hospital stay. The other students, long disgruntled at seeing top honors go to a foreigner, rallied around their classmate Brown, whose grades were next in line. "This is your chance!" they told him. "Kikuchi's sick and can't take lecture notes, so you've got to defend British pride and become head of the class!"

In time Kikuchi recovered and sat for the final examination. When the term grades were posted, his name was first, Brown's second. Upon seeing this, Brown murmured to himself in satisfaction, "I saved British honor." It turned out that Brown had visited Kikuchi in the hospital and taken him his lecture notes.

In a world where all too often people wish misfortune on others and take pleasure in the failures of their supposed friends, what an inspiring example of true friendship! In a world that laughs at others' woes, it is precisely such truly gentlemanly conduct that is most worth preserving.

62

When Everyone Is in the Wrong, No Quarrels

The Secret of a Happy Home Life

A family that was always at loggerheads lived side by side with a family that was as peaceful as could be. A, the head of the quarrelsome family, was mystified by how well everyone got along next door. Finally one day he called on B and said in desperation, "Our family is always quarreling, as I'm sure you can tell, and I don't know what to do about it. I see that everyone in your family gets along beautifully. Please tell me what your secret is."

B replied, "There's no secret in particular. It's probably because everyone in your family is always in the right. Over here, all of us are always in the wrong, so there's no quarreling. That's all there is to it."

Certain that he was being ridiculed, A was about to explode in anger when a loud crash sounded from inside the house. It sounded as if a piece of crockery had fallen to the floor.

The voice of a young woman said penitently, "Mother, I'm so sorry. All because I didn't look where I was going, I went and broke that dish that meant so much to you. It's my fault. Please forgive me."

"Nonsense," said the voice of her mother-in-law. "It's not your fault at all. I kept meaning to put the dish away, and never got around to it. I never should have left it there in the first place. I'm the one who has to apologize."

Then it dawned on A: "I get it. Everyone in this family is always in the wrong, and says so. That's why there's no quarreling."

I cannot condemn others
    though their sins be red as wine,
For truly their offenses pale
    next to those of mine.

63

What Tastes Best; What Tastes Worst

The Ingredients of Happiness

Tokugawa Ieyasu (1542–1616), the founder and first shogun of the Tokugawa shogunate, once gathered a few stalwart men around him and, after having each one speak of his feats in battle, asked them to name the best-tasting thing in the world. One said wine, another sweets, still another fruit. They disputed the matter, each man sticking up for his personal favorite, but Ieyasu did not appear satisfied.

Finally he turned to his trusted attendant, a woman named Okaji, and asked, "What do you say is the best-tasting thing in the world?"

Okaji smiled and answered tersely, "Salt."

For the first time, Ieyasu gave a smile of satisfaction. He followed this up with another question: "And the worst-tasting thing?"

She replied nonchalantly, "The worst-tasting thing is also salt."

Ieyasu was amazed at her wisdom.

The undeniable truth of Okaji's answer is based on the following principles. Because salt enhances all other flavors, it is surely the best-tasting thing in the world. Likewise, because salt ruins all other flavors, it is also the worst-tasting thing in the world. Of course salt itself is neither pleasant to the taste nor otherwise; its effect is a matter of proportion. Salt is just one ingredient of flavor, and knowing how to use it in proportion is all.

Health, wealth, reputation, and status are all mere ingredients of happiness. The key to true well-being is being able to manage them capably.

64

Change Yourself, and Others Will Follow

The Samurai and the Horse

When the Zen priest Bankei (1622–93) was still an acolyte, every night he would sit in meditation. One morning after meditating he was resting by a stable when a samurai came along to train his horse. As Bankei looked on idly, it became apparent to him that the horse was out of sorts, and balking at its rider's commands. The samurai yelled at the animal and beat it.

Bankei shouted, "What do you think you're doing!"

The samurai paid no attention, but only whipped the animal all the harder. Bankei kept on shouting, until finally the samurai dismounted and walked over to him.

"You have been scolding me for some time, I believe," he said quietly. "If you have something to teach me, I am willing to listen." His words were exceedingly polite, but it was clear that depending on what kind of answer he received, he might erupt in anger.

Without hesitating, Bankei told him, "It is foolish to blame only the horse for failing to listen to you. The horse has its own reasons. If you want it to listen, you must encourage it to do so. To do that, you must start with yourself. Do you understand?"

This was a humble and intelligent samurai, for he nodded, bowed, and left. Then, with a change of attitude, he remounted his steed. Sure enough, the horse too was now a changed creature, and docilely obeyed his every command.

People constantly blame others for their own faults, and find no peace. The essential thing is to take an honest look at oneself and correct one's own attitude. Do that, and others will change too. Your home life is guaranteed to be happier.

65

Success Is the Fruit of Effort

The Astute Merchant

Long ago, there were two merchants who always crossed a narrow mountain pass with dry goods loaded on their backs.

One day, one of them plopped down on a rock by the roadside. "Exhausting, isn't it?" he sighed. "Let's rest for a while. You know, if only this pass weren't so high, we could cross it easily and make more money." He looked up balefully at the steep pass.

"I disagree," replied his companion. "In fact, I wish this pass were higher and steeper."

"You do?" said the first man in astonishment. "Whatever for? Do you enjoy suffering? How strange!"

His companion explained, "If this pass were easy to cross, everybody would use it to do business, and our profits would go down; if it were higher and steeper, no one but us would cross it, and our business would prosper even more."

Successful tradesmen must be not only astute in business, but bold in endeavor. Success is the fruit of one's effort. All that comes easily is poverty and shame.

The harder the task, the more glorious the triumph.

About the Author

KENTETSU TAKAMORI is a Pure Land Buddhist teacher born in Japan in 1929. He has lectured throughout Japan and worldwide on Buddhism for more than half a century. He is the author of several best-selling titles in Japanese and the chair of the Buddhist organization Jodo Shinshu Shinrankai.

YOU WERE BORN FOR A REASON: *The Real Purpose of Life* was the first of his works to be published in English (Ichimannendo Publishing, Inc., 2006). This is a translation of the book *Naze ikiru* (Ichimannendo Publishing, 2001), which has sold over 600,000 copies to date.

His life has been dedicated to faithfully conveying the teachings of Shinran (1173–1263), the founder of Shin Buddhism (the True Pure Land School).

He lives with his wife and their dog in a small town in Toyama Prefecture overlooking the Japan Sea.

To the Reader

Please take a minute to share your thoughts with us.
We want to know how the stories in this book affected you.
Which were your favorites, and why?
Your comments will be helpful in planning future titles.
Please email us at info@i-ipi.com

Or write us at Ichimannendo Publishing, Inc. (IPI),
19750 S. Vermont Ave., Suite 200, Torrance, CA 90502

For more information on this and other books by
Ichimannendo Publishing, Inc., please visit our website at
www.i-ipi.com